rockschool®

Piano

US Level 4 (UK Grade 4)

Performance pieces, technical exercises, supporting tests and in-depth guidance for Rockschool assessments

All accompanying and supporting audio can be downloaded from: *www.rslawards.com/downloads*

Input the following code when prompted: **8FAT3XYSZ2**

For more information, turn to page 5

Acknowledgements

Published by Rockschool Ltd. © 2019 & 2020
Catalogue Number: RSK200093US
ISBN: 978-1-78936-169-8
Initial US Release | Errata details can be found at *www.rslawards.com/errata*

SYLLABUS
Syllabus designed and written by Jono Harrison
Syllabus Director: Tim Bennett-Hart
Syllabus consultants: Gary Sanctuary, Chris Stanbury, Simon Troup and Jennie Troup
Hit Tune arrangements by Jono Harrison and Gary Sanctuary
Supporting Tests written by Jono Harrison, Chris Stanbury, Nik Preston and Ash Preston
Syllabus advisors: Tim Bennett-Hart, Brian Ashworth, Stuart Slater, Peter Huntington, Bruce Darlington, Simon Troup and Jennie Troup

PUBLISHING
Proof reading of arrangements by Sharon Kelly, Simon Troup, Jennie Troup and Jono Harrison
Music engraving and book layout by Simon and Jennie Troup of Digital Music Art
Fact files written and edited by Abbie Thomas
Notes written by Roland Perrin
Proof reading and copy editing by Gemma Bull, Jono Harrison and Jennie Troup
Cover design by Philip Millard of Rather Nice Design
Cover photograph: © Nomad_Soul (Shutterstock)

AUDIO
Produced by Jono Harrison
Engineered by Jono Harrison, Gary Sanctuary, Tim Bennett-Hart, Pete Riley, Richard Brook, Rory Harvey and Andy Robertson
Assisted by Paul Pritchard at Abbey Road
Recorded at Dock Street Studios, The Dairy and Abbey Road
Mixed by Patrick Phillips
Mastered by Francis Gorini

Supporting Tests recorded by Chris Stanbury and Jono Harrison

MUSICIANS
Piano and Keyboards: Jono Harrison, Gary Sanctuary, Ross Stanley & Tania Ilyashova
Drums & Percussion: Pete Riley and Richard Brook
Bass & Synth Bass: Andy Robertson
Guitars: Rory Harvey, Nat Martin and Jono Harrison
Saxophone: Jonathan Griffiths
Trombone: Tom George White and Norton York
Trumpet: Nick Mead and John Simpson
Lead and Backing Vocals: Glen Harvey & Katie Hector
Additional Programming: Jono Harrison

DISTRIBUTION
Exclusive Distributors: Hal Leonard

CONTACTING ROCKSCHOOL
www.rslawards.com
Telephone: +44 (0)345 460 4747
Email: *info@rslawards.com*

EXECUTIVE PRODUCERS
John Simpson, Norton York

RSL Awarding the Contemporary Arts

Table of Contents

Welcome to Rockschool Piano Level/Grade 4

Welcome to Rockschool's Piano syllabus 2019. This syllabus is designed to support pianists in their progression from Debut to Level/Grade 8, through an engaging and rigorous pathway covering all the genres, stylistic elements, techniques and musical skills required for success as a contemporary pianist.

Piano Assessments
At each level/grade you have the option of taking one of two different types of assessment:

- Level/**Grade Assessment**
  A Level/Grade Assessment is a mixture of music performances, technical work and tests. You are required to prepare three pieces (two of which may be Free Choice Pieces) and the contents of the Technical Exercise section. This accounts for 75% of the assessment marks. The other 25% consists of: either a Sight Reading or an Improvisation & Interpretation test (10%), two Ear Tests (10%), and finally you will be asked five General Musicianship Questions (5%). The pass mark is 60%.

- **Performance Certificate**
  A Performance Certificate is equivalent to a Level/Grade Assessment, but in a Performance Certificate you are required to perform five pieces. A maximum of three of these can be Free Choice Pieces. Each song is marked out of 20 and the pass mark is 60%.

All elements required to participate in a Rockschool assessment can be found in the level/grade book. These are as follows:

- **Assessment Pieces**
  The 2019 syllabus comprises six 'hit tune' arrangements, benchmarked and devised so as to equip contemporary pianists with industry-relevant skills in any performance environment. These fall into three categories:

  Melody & Accompaniment
  These arrangements are performed to full band backing tracks, with the piano performing both melody and accompaniment

  Solo Piano Arrangement
  These are full solo piano arrangements, performed without backing tracks

  Vocal Accompaniment
  These arrangements cover the skills required of contemporary pianists in ensemble environments, be they on the stage or in the studio. The backing tracks feature vocalists, and the piano parts are reflective of what session pianists would perform live or on mainstream commercial recordings

  Each 'hit tune' arrangement is preceded by a Fact File, giving surrounding context to the piece and the original performers/recording artists.

  Furthermore, at the end of each arrangement you will find notes giving additional supportive context to get the most out of the pieces.

- **Technical Exercises**
  There are either three or four groups of technical exercise, depending on the level/grade:

  Debut–Level/Grade 8:
  Group A: Scales
  Group B: Arpeggios/Broken Chords
  Group C: Chord Voicings

  Levels/Grades 4–8 only:
  Group D: Technical Study

- **Supporting Tests**
  There are three types of unprepared supporting tests in the assessment:

  1. The first type can be one of two options (this is the *candidate's* choice):

     Either:
     Sight Reading tests, developing the musician's ability to read and perform previously unseen material;

     or:
     Improvisation & Interpretation tests, developing the musician's ability to develop previously unseen material in a stylistic way and perform improvised passages of melody. The book contains examples of both types of test – equivalent 'unseen' examples will be provided for the assessment

  2. **Ear Tests**
     Debut–Level/Grade 3: feature Melodic Recall and Chord Recognition
     Levels/Grades 4–8: feature Melodic Recall and Harmonic Recall

  3. **General Musicianship Questions (GMQs)**, which you will be asked by the assessor at the end of each assessment

General Information
You will find information on assessment procedures, including online assessment entry, marking schemes, information on Free Choice Pieces and improvisation requirements for each level/grade.

Audio
In addition to the level/grade book, we have also provided audio in the form of backing tracks (minus piano) and full tracks (including piano) for all 'hit tune' arrangements, technical exercises and supporting tests (where applicable). We have provided professional performance recordings of all solo piano pieces in the syllabus. This audio can be downloaded from RSL directly at *www.rslawards.com/downloads*

You will need to input this code when prompted: **8FAT3XYSZ2**

The audio files are supplied in MP3 format. Once downloaded you will be able to play them on any compatible device.

Further Information
You can find further details about Rockschool's Contemporary Piano syllabus by downloading the syllabus guide from our website: *www.rslawards.com*

All candidates should download and read the accompanying syllabus guide when using this level/grade book.

Performance and Technical Guidance

Fingering
Any fingering annotation is given as a guide only.

Interpretation
Notation should be performed exactly as written, except where there are performance indications to ad. lib, improvise, develop, etc. In these instances, the candidate will be marked on their ability to interpret the music in a stylistically appropriate way, commensurate with the level.

Adaptation
A small degree of adaptation is allowed where, for example, hand stretches do not facilitate the required notated parts. Marks may be deducted if adaptation results in over-simplification of the notation. If in doubt you can submit any adaptation enquiries to *info@rslawards.com*

Articulation & Dynamics
Where articulation and dynamics are marked on the notation, they should be followed. Where it is open to interpretation, the candidate is free to take their own approach.

Pedalling
The candidate may use the pedal freely at any level/grade, but it should be applied judiciously as marks may be deducted for any over usage resulting in an unclear tone. In addition, where pedalling is written into (or out of) the notation, this should be observed.

Chord Symbols
Most hit tune arrangements have chord symbols written above the notation. This is purely for guidance, and to assist the candidate and teacher.

All Of Me

SONG TITLE: 'ALL OF ME'
ALBUM: LOVE IN THE FUTURE
RELEASED: 2013
LABEL: COLUMBIA
GENRE: R&B/SOUL/POP
WRITTEN BY: JOHN STEPHENS/TOBY GAD
PRODUCED BY: DAVE TOZER/JOHN LEGEND
US CHART PEAK: 1

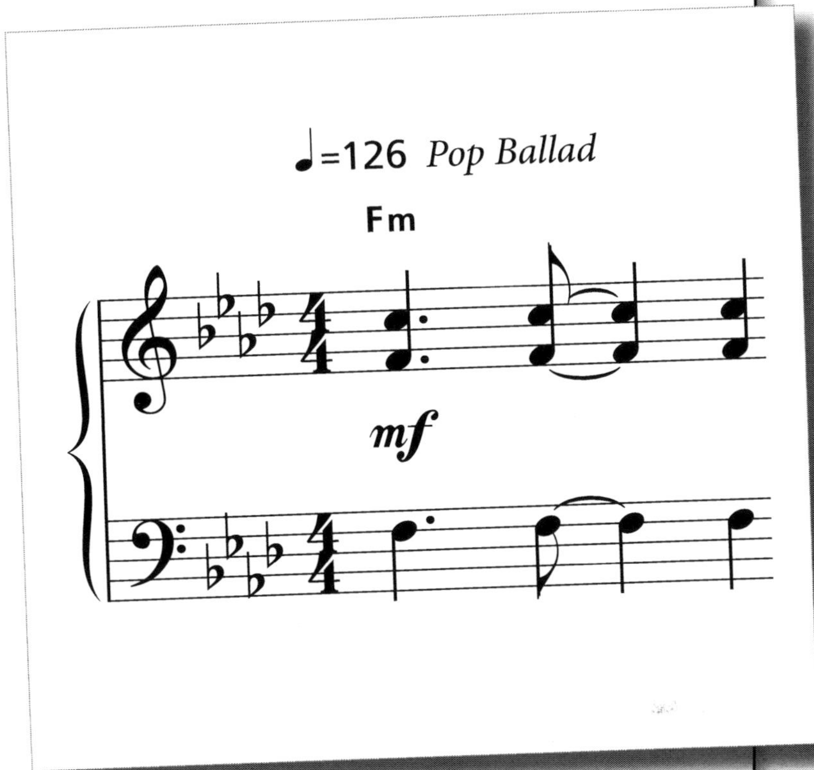

'All of Me' was the third single to be released from John Legend's fourth studio album, *Love in the Future.* The song was written as a tribute to Legend's then Fiancée (and now wife) Chrissy Teigen, whom he met in 2007 on the set of his video for 'Stereo'. Legend achieved global success with the single, peaking at number 2 in the UK and topping the charts in the US by knocking Pharrell Williams' 'Happy' off the top spot after a ten-week reign. 'All of Me' also proved to be a hit in Australia, Canada, Ireland, Portugal, Sweden, Switzerland and The Netherlands, in all of which it topped the singles charts. At the end of 2014 it was announced that Williams' 'Happy' was the best-selling song of the year, followed closely by none other than 'All of Me' in second place with 4.67 million sales for the year.

John Legend was born John Roger Stephens in 1978 in Ohio, where he was one of four children. At the age of just four years old Legend was already performing with his church choir and took up the piano at the young age of seven. After graduating from High School Legend went on to study English at the University of Pennsylvania, where he served as the president and musical director of a co-ed jazz and pop a cappella group called Counterparts. The group were so successful that Legend's name became known and no sooner was he being introduced to global superstar Lauryn Hill. Hill hired Legend to play on her song 'Everything is Everything' and this led to the start of a brilliant musical career.

Whilst working on songwriting and demo recordings to send out to record producers, Legend was introduced to the up and coming star Kanye West. Shortly after performing some session vocals for West, Legend found himself signing to West's label and soon released his debut studio album *Get Lifted (2004).*

Although a worldwide success, John Legend had to wait a long time for his first chart topper. 'All of Me' was his first US number 1 single, ten years after releasing his debut album. A fact which seems inconceivable when researching his past work and achievements. To date, John Legend has won an impressive ten Grammy Awards, as well as an Academy Award for 'Best Original Song'. Although he waited a long time to receive the recognition he deserved, it is evident that he is now viewed in the industry as an incredibly talented songwriter and musician.

All Of Me

John Legend

D♭maj7
A♭
E♭
[14]
Fm
D♭
A♭sus4
A♭
E♭
[17]
B
B♭m
mf
A♭
E♭
[21]
B♭m
A♭
E♭
[25]

A♭
Fmadd9
[29]
D♭6
E♭9sus4
E♭
[33]
A♭
Fmadd9
[37]
D♭6
E♭9sus4
E♭
[41]

C
Fm
D♭
A♭
E♭
dolce
[45]
To Coda
E♭5
[49]
D♭maj7
mf
[53]
D.%. al Coda
[57]
Coda
p
[61]

Notes

There is a powerful theme of romance behind this composition, emphasised by both a persistent rhythmic pulse (as seen in the stark open chordal rhythms of measures 1–4), versus flowing arpeggio lines between both hands (measures 29–30, for example). Throughout the performance there should be a strong sense of the quarter-note pulse in the measure, and the teacher can encourage the pupil to internalise this by tapping one foot to the pulse during practice.

Care is also needed to make sure that the song's melody is projected clearly. From letter A until the end, the top part should sing out louder than the accompaniment, and a good method is to practise the melody in sections on its own. It can also help to experiment with the accompaniment in isolation, balancing the chord tones and arpeggios against the lowest bass notes. Note that at certain points the melody is accompanied by a weaving constant eighth-note figure, for example measures 25 and 29–32. The student must be clear which notes are melody and which are accompaniment within these patterns, and studying the original recording will help achieve this.

If the student finds the independence of the hands challenging at times, it can be helpful to 'loop' a measure playing just the left hand part. They might then add beat 1 of the right hand part to the loop, then the second beat, building up the measure and section in this way. The direct emotional intensity of this song will only be portrayed when the student is completely familiar with the music. Practising in sections slowly will help here, steadily increasing the tempo as the technical stability develops. It is important to understand not only the details of each measure, but how the wider sections play a role within the composition.

SONG TITLE: 'RESPECT'
ALBUM: I NEVER LOVED A MAN THE WAY I LOVE YOU
RELEASED: 1967
LABEL: ATLANTIC
GENRE: SOUL
WRITTEN BY: OTIS REDDING
PRODUCED BY: JERRY WEXLER
US CHART PEAK: 1

'Respect' was written and originally released by Motown legend Otis Redding in 1965. Although Redding achieved significant success with the song, it became more famously known as a global hit for iconic vocalist Aretha Franklin. Redding's original intention of the song tells the story of a hardworking man bringing money home to his abiding housewife. However, Franklin flips this on its head and delivers a lyric describing a strong and independent woman. Many have viewed the original as misogynistic, while Franklin's version has been cited as a landmark for the feminist movement – quite a contrast. The hugely famous R-E-S-P-E-C-T middle eight was actually added by Franklin herself, with her backing singers responding with the well-known reply "sock it to me…".

Aretha Franklin was an incredibly talented woman and lent her hand to many courageous roles, such as singer, songwriter, actress, pianist and civil rights activist. Her love for music began at a very young age, singing gospel at the church where her father was minister in her hometown. At 18 years old she signed for Columbia records, recording secular music and achieving minor success. It was on signing with Atlantic Records in 1966 that Franklin achieved global success, with hits such as 'Respect', 'Chain of Fools', 'Think' and '(You Make Me Feel Like a) Natural Woman' (to name a few). The singer soon became widely known as "The Queen of Soul".

Franklin sadly passed away in August 2018 at the age of 76, but left behind an unbelievable legacy. Not only did she record 112 Billboard charting singles, but she also became the first female performer to be inducted into the Rock and Roll Hall of Fame in 1987. She has inspired thousands with her incredible vocal and stunning interpretation of endless hits. In 2008 Rolling Stone Magazine actually ranked Franklin as the number 1 greatest singer of all time, a position very much deserved.

'Respect' sent Franklin flying into success, topping the Billboard charts and peaking at number 10 in the UK. It sold well over 1 million copies and went on to be listed by Rolling Stone magazine as the 5th greatest song of all time. Throughout her career Franklin received a mesmerising 44 Grammy nominations, 18 of which she won, including nominations for Best R&B Vocal Performance (Female) for ten years running between 1974 and 1984. Had it not been for her iconic version of 'Respect' we may never have known the legend that was Aretha Franklin.

Respect

Aretha Franklin

Words & Music by Otis Redding

C7
F
C7
F
To Coda
[21]
C
F♯m
B
[25]
F♯m
G7
D.𝄋. al Coda
[29]
Coda
D
C7
F
C7
F
[33]
E
C7
F
C7
[37]
F
C7
F
Rit.
C7
[40]

Notes

Students will need to have a solid understanding of the music's rhythmic vocabulary to help build a secure and confident performance.

Before playing any of the notes, students should lightly tap the quarter note pulse at a medium tempo with one foot. Then they can vocalise a measure of 16th note subdivisions, for example by saying 'ta-ka-ta-ka' or '1-e-&-a 2-e-&-a 3-e-&-a 4-e-&-a'. With regular work on this rhythmic foundation, teachers can help students understand how different 16th note rhythms fit together later on, as found in this piece.

To practise the opening, students can clap composite rhythms of first two measures – then tap them out as they are split between both hands. Students will now be ready to slowly put together the first four measures of the piano part.

Letter A and B present different rhythmic challenges to the opening measures, with inventive right hand chordal work and more pronounced bass rhythms in the left. The quarter-note pulse and the overlaying 16th-note subdivision still need to be kept in mind. The groove in these measures must be, as funk musicians call it, *in the pocket*.

The groove intensifies subtly between measure 21 and 24, and will need careful attention. The 16th-note phrase in the bass line needs to be *legato*, and played with full weight.

Teachers should guide students to make a real contrast at letter C, where the music is *forte* and sustained in both hands.

In the coda, it is very important to play the single eighth-note chords crisply, carefully articulating the rests. The 16th note bass line needs to be played with the same *legato* phrasing as before.

SONG TITLE: LET IT GO
ALBUM: FROZEN
RELEASED: 2013
LABEL: WALT DISNEY
GENRE: MUSICAL THEATRE
VOCALS: IDINA MENZEL
ORCHESTRATION: DAVE METZGER
WRITTEN BY: KRISTEN ANDERSON-LOPEZ, ROBERT LOPEZ
PRODUCED BY: KRISTEN ANDERSON-LOPEZ, ROBERT LOPEZ, CHRISTOPHE BECK, CHRIS MONTAN, TOM MACDOUGALL
US CHART PEAK: 5

This song represents a defining moment in the Disney animated film, *Frozen*, for Queen Elsa; the moment she realises she no longer has to hide her abilities and is now free from the restrictive childhood she endured trying to keep her powers secret. 'Let It Go' has won both an Oscar and a Grammy and has become one of the biggest selling singles of all time.

The song was apparently written in a single day, with the husband and wife songwriting team (Kirsten Anderson-Lopez & Robert Lopez) improvising on the piano whilst brainstorming lyrical ideas. The piano and vocal score was then sent to orchestrator and composer, Dave Metzger, who created the orchestral score. Metzger is also known for his work on Disney's 1999 adaption of *Tarzan*, as well as Box Office hits *Armageddon* and *Hancock* (to name a few).

It has been said that the song itself caused a rewriting of the movie to ensure that Queen Elsa became one of the main characters and was written as a far more complex and vulnerable character; she was originally meant to appear as a villain. The story is based on the Hans Christian Anderson tale *The Snow Queen*. Script-writer and Director Jennifer Lee said she had used the film and its strong female characters to inspire her own daughter, who had been bullied at school. Jennifer Lee has been known for having to flit between people who said they loved the film to apologising for the number of times in which their children have incessantly listened to the songs and watched the movie.

Frozen has won two Oscars (one of which was for this song), two BAFTAs and two Grammys. It has earned nearly $1.3 billion dollars at the box office and has become the highest grossing animated film to date.

Let It Go

Kristen Anderson-Lopez and Robert Lopez

From 'Frozen' (2013)

Fm
E♭
B♭
[11]
B
E♭
D♭
[13]
E♭
D♭
[15]
C
A♭
E♭
Fm
D♭
mf
Cross LH over RH
p
[18]
A♭
E♭
Fm
D♭
(cross LH over RH)
[20]

A♭
E♭
Fm
D♭
(cross LH over RH)
[22]
Cm
C♭
D♭
(cross LH over RH)
[24]
D
A♭
E♭/G
Fm
D♭
mf
[26]
E♭
B♭m
Fm
E♭
[28]
B♭sus4
B♭
E♭
[30]
D♭
E♭
[32]

D♭
[34]
E
A♭
E♭
Fm
D♭
f
[36]
A♭
E♭
Fm
D♭
[38]
A♭
E♭
Fm
D♭
[40]
D♭m7
Cm
C♭
ff
subito p
[42]
D♭add 9
[44]

Notes

The opening syncopated rhythms might need to be practised slowly, one measure at a time. Once the notes have been mastered, a light touch is required to achieve the right effect.

The 'sung' melody begins at Letter A, and, although still at a *piano* dynamic, it should project more strongly than the introduction of the piece.

Throughout the song, the melody should be given plenty of light and shade. Teachers should guide students with how to bring the top line alive with careful use of shaping and phrasing ideas. This can be helped by listening to the original and studying how the vocalist adds emphasis and articulation to certain lines.

At letter C, where the hands cross over, the top part can be thought of as a music box. A clear, bell like tone is required at this point.

Students must ensure that the left hand is *staccato* in the first four measures of letter D, and slightly quieter than the right hand melody. Staccato does not mean accented!

Be aware that the sudden *piano* at the end begins on the last 16th note in measure 43 to coincide with the final vocal line. This is a dramatic compositional effect which brings an abrupt but satisfying close to the piece.

Goodbye Yellow Brick Road

SONG TITLE: 'GOODBYE YELLOW BRICK ROAD'
ALBUM: GOODBYE YELLOW BRICK ROAD
RELEASED: 1973
LABEL: MCA/DJM
GENRE: SOFT ROCK/GLAM ROCK
WRITTEN BY: ELTON JOHN/ BERNIE TAUPIN
PRODUCED BY: GUS DUDGEON
US CHART PEAK: 2

'Goodbye Yellow Brick Road' was the second single to be released from Elton John's seventh studio album of the same name. The single hit the charts in 1973 and quickly surpassed the success of his previous single 'Saturday Night's Alright for Fighting', making it to the top ten in both the UK and US singles charts. By January 1974 the song had reached gold status in the US, only to be re-certified as platinum in 1995.

With Elton John writing the music and Bernie Taupin the lyrics, the song was sure to be a commercial hit. Taupin's lyrics are inspired by the classic story of 'The Wizard of Oz'. The 1939 adaption was the first film Taupin ever saw and so its plot remained somewhat nostalgic to the writer. John sings of wanting to return to his roots and to a simpler time, similar to the character of Dorothy who follows the yellow brick road in her quest to get back home.

The duo received excellent reviews for their latest hit, with many claiming that it was John's best release yet. Allmusic described the track as a "vocal triumph" and a "pinnacle of its style", with other music critics praising it for its delicacy and beauty. The album on which the song features, also named *Goodbye Yellow Brick Road,* was also met by critical acclaim and is regarded as John's most successful and recognisable work. On its release in 1973 it entered the US album chart at number 17, before climbing to the top spot where it stayed for eight weeks. In 2003 the album was inducted into the Grammy Hall of Fame and was ranked number 91 on Rolling Stone magazine's 'The 500 Greatest Albums of all Time' list. With sales of over 8 million copies in the US, the iconic album is now certified 8xPlatinum.

Elton John and Bernie Taupin are one of the most successful writing teams of the 20th Century, their work includes smash hits 'Candle in the Wind', 'Bennie and the Jets' and 'Crocodile Rock' to name just a few. Their working partnership is highly regarded in the music industry, with many fans thriving to know more about the pair. Taupin has published several books about his time working with Elton, including 'Bernie Taupin: The One Who Writes the Words for Elton John' which is actually a collection of all of his work for the album *Goodbye Yellow Brick Road.*

Goodbye Yellow Brick Road

Elton John

Words by Bernie Taupin
Music by Elton John

C7 C7/E F F/A B♭ B♭/F
[14]
E♭ E♭/B♭ C C/E F
[17]
B
B♭m B♭m/F E♭ E♭/G A♭ A♭/C
f
[21]
D♭ D♭/C B♭m B♭m/F C C/G
[24]

C
F
A7
B♭
mf
[27]
F
F/C
D7
Gm
[30]
C7
F
F/E
Dm
[33]
A7
A7/E
B♭
D♭
E♭
[36]

F
F/E
Dm
Dm/C
B♭
C
[40]
D
B♭m
B♭m/F
E♭
E♭/G
A♭
A♭/C
f
[43]
1.
2.
D♭
D♭/C
B♭m
B♭m/F
C
B♭m
B♭m/F
[46]
Rit.
F
p
[50]

Notes

As with all the greatest pop songs, the lyrics of this song are as important as the music. This arrangement presents students with a particular challenge: to make this instrumental version as convincing as the vocal one.

Teachers might recommend that students can achieve this in the following ways:

- Ensure that the melody sings out and is played significantly stronger than the accompaniment. This will require understanding which notes in the right hand take the melody line. For example: in measure 6, the notes with the stems pointing downwards are accompaniment. The whole of measure 12 is also accompaniment. Careful study of the original recording will help students become familiar with this.
- Dynamic contrasts are very important in this song. This is particularly true at letter B: students should make sure they observe the *crescendo* leading into this section, and also the *diminuendo* at the end of it.

To help navigate the key changes, it is recommended that students become very familiar with the scales of F major and A♭ major.

Attention needs to be paid to the right hand part in measures 9 to 11. Here, it is required that the notes are played one octave lower than written.

The song effectively finishes in measure 51, but the discipline of holding the final chord and counting silently up to the end of 53 is important.

I See Fire

SONG TITLE: I SEE FIRE
ALBUM: THE HOBBIT: THE DESOLATION OF SMAUG, X (ED SHEERAN)
RELEASED: 2013
LABEL: WATERTOWER MUSIC, DECCA
GENRE: FOLK
WRITTEN BY: ED SHEERAN, CHARLIE MILNER
PRODUCED BY: ED SHEERAN
US CHART PEAK: N/A

This song featured on the soundtrack of the 2013 film *The Hobbit: The Desolation of Smaug*, appearing at the end credits. The film's producer, Peter Jackson, chose Sheeran because his daughter was a fan of the singer. Ed agreed to write for the film due to his childhood connection with the books; the first book he had ever read was *The Hobbit*. He also enjoyed the *Lord of the Rings Trilogy* by author J.R.R. Tolkein and was a fan of Peter Jackson's movies based on the books. In the space of one day, Ed saw the film, wrote, and recorded the song. The song, according to Jackson, is Sheeran's emotional response to the film and says that he was advised by Jackson to "write a song that takes the audience by the hand and lead them from Middle Earth back into reality."

Notably, Sheeran plays most of the instruments on the track and says: "I got the chance to produce and play all the instruments on it apart from the cello, and I managed to learn the violin for a day." Sheeran did dictate the cello part to the cellist, however, despite not playing it himself.

The song is inspired by Celtic folk sounds as Peter Jackson had suggested that Sheeran write something within the folk genre. The lyrics of the ballad tell a story, based on Sheeran's attempts to understand the experience and feelings of the characters in the final scenes of the film.

In 2010, despite not having any gigs booked, Sheeran bought himself a plane ticket to Los Angeles and set off in the hope of launching his music career. He played several open-mic nights before being spotted by actor Jamie Foxx. Foxx was so impressed he gave Sheeran the use of his recording studio and let him stay in his Hollywood home for the rest of his trip. Sheeran has won five BRIT awards and four Ivor Novello Awards. He has been nominated for an astonishing 13 Grammy's, four of which he won. His career reached new heights when he was appointed an MBE in 2017 for his services to music and charity.

I See Fire

Ed Sheeran

From 'The Hobbit: The Desolation of Smaug' (2013)

Bm D A Gmaj7
3
[9]
Em7 F♯m G
[11]
Bm G A Bm
[13]
B
Bm D A Gmaj7
[15]
Bm D A Em7
3
3
[17]

Bm7 D A Gmaj7
3
[19]
Em7 F♯m G
3
[21]
Emadd9 F♯m G
[23]
C
Bm7 Gadd9 A Bm7
stronger
[25]
Bm7 Gadd9 A Bm7
[27]

Bm7
Gadd9
A
Bm7
[29]
Gadd9
A
Em7
1.
Emadd9
[31]
D
Bm
G
A
Bm
[34]
G
A
Bm
mf
[36]
2.
Emadd9
[38]

Notes

This song has a quiet, understated feeling, but should still be played with a steady groove. In preparation and practice, students could lightly tap the quarter note pulse with a foot at slower tempos and/or along with a metronome, before moving up to full tempo to play along to the backing track.

The opening right hand phrase was originally played on the guitar. On the piano, it can be slightly awkward if not prepared properly. Fingering preference can differ on phrases such as these, so experimentation is important. Students may wish to play the opening diad with 1 & 4, leaving them in a strong position for the faster F♯-E-D run (5, 4, 3). They might then wish to take the lower notes A & B both with 1, to ensure they can move back up to position to play the final D, F♯ and G with 1, 4 & 5.

The grace notes in measures 2 and 4 should be omitted until the phrase can be played confidently: this is a guitar phrase, and the articulation is characteristic of that instrument.

Students should have an awareness about which part of the song is 'sung' melody and which is instrumental interlude. Teachers might discuss with students about how this could affect interpretation, and should guide students in ensuring a difference between the two parts.

The vocal line is from the last beat and a half of measure 4, to the end of measure 12. It returns on last beat and a half of measure 14, to the end of measure 33. The 2nd time ending is also sung. The rest of the song is instrumental.

Students should be encouraged to bring out the chorus at letter D, but without disturbing the overall peacefulness of the song.

Livin' On A Prayer

SONG TITLE: 'LIVIN' ON A PRAYER'
ALBUM: SLIPPERY WHEN WET
RELEASED: 1986
LABEL: MERCURY
GENRE: HARD ROCK/GLAM METAL
WRITTEN BY: JON BON JOVI/RICHIE SAMBORA/DESMOND CHILD
PRODUCED BY: BRUCE FAIRBAIRN
US CHART PEAK: 1

'Livin' On a Prayer' was a 1986 hit for multi-million selling rock band Bon Jovi. The track was the second single to be released from their third studio album, *Slippery When Wet,* and gave them their second consecutive US number 1 single preceded by the iconic 'You Give Love a Bad Name'. Bon Jovi's hit was well received around the globe, topping the charts in Canada, New Zealand and Norway as well as the US, peaking at number 4 on the UK singles chart and achieving top ten status in Australia, Belgium, Finland, Ireland, the Netherlands, South Africa, Spain and Sweden.

'Livin' On a Prayer' was written by Bon Jovi's frontman Jon Bon Jovi, then guitarist Richie Sambora and renowned songwriter Desmond Child. On first recording the song, the prestigious frontman was unhappy with the result and wanted to scrap the song, but Sambora persuaded him to persevere saying that they had simply approached it wrong. Instrument parts were changed and re-recorded and the band finally agreed that the song should feature on their up and coming album, *Slippery When Wet.* This decision certainly paid off, with the song originally marking physical sales of 800,000 on its release and later being certified 3 x Platinum in 2013 for over 3 million digital downloads.

Slippery When Wet was met with positive reviews and reached number 6 in the UK album chart. It produced a further third successful single release with 'Wanted Dead or Alive', giving the band three consecutive US top ten hits. The album has now been certified Diamond in the US, with sales of over 12 million copies and was ranked 44th in the Rock and Roll Hall of Fame's list 'Definitive 200 Albums of All Time'. Bon Jovi have released thirteen studio albums to date, and with five of them topping the UK album charts they are clearly an asset to the commercial world of rock music. In 1996 they won Best International Group at the annual Brit awards, confirming their importance in the 90s rock scene.

Although the line-up has changed since their formation in 1983, Bon Jovi continue to tour worldwide and plans for a 2019 global tour are well underway. The band have performed over 2,700 times in more than 50 countries and have sold over 100 million records worldwide, making them one of the best-selling American rock bands of all time.

Livin' On A Prayer

Bon Jovi

[12]
[15]
B
mf
[19]
[23]
C
f
[27]

[30]
[33]
D
[37]
[40]
subito p
[43]

mf
[46]
E
f
[50]
[53]
[56]
[59]

Notes

This is quintessential rock music arranged for solo piano, and needs to be performed with all the drama and power associated with the style.

The famous introductory bass and guitar figure (or 'riff') taken by the left hand at measures 1 and 2 needs to be clear and precise – this is one of the most iconic parts of the song. Students can practise how best to articulate this passage, experimenting with the 'weight' and duration of the notes.

At letter A, the left-hand part plays a more supportive role to the right, with chord tone roots and octaves in a simple and supportive rhythmic pattern, allowing space for the melody. The right hand carries both the vocal line and chord tones, to add richness to the texture. It is important to achieve a balance so melody takes precedence.

For this piano arrangement, *mezzo piano* is indicated dynamic in the introduction and A section in order to allow more contrast with the latter sections of the piece. Note how a brief but well-judged *crescendo* (measure 18 beats 3 & 4) will set up the *mezzo forte* dynamic of section B. It is important not to over emphasise this shift, as there needs to be headroom for the chorus *forte* dynamic at section C.

Quarter-note triplets feature at various places in the piece, and to become familiar with this rhythm it can be a helpful exercise to tap a quarter-note pulse with the foot, whilst clapping six quarter-note triplets evenly within each measure of four.

The original guitar solo is re-interpreted for solo piano from letter D (measure 37), and should be treated with the same approach to projection as the melody. For impact, a sudden *piano* dynamic drop occurs in measure 44, setting up the climax of the solo over a *crescendo* through to measure 46. Care is needed to ensure a measure of three beats is counted at measure 49, a time signature 'trick' which adds weight to the impact of the key change in the following measure. Familiarity with both G major and B♭ major scales (and their related pentatonics) will ensure that these passages can be navigated successfully.

Finally, maintaining an internal count is important right through the final measures, ensuring that the final chord is held for the duration indicated.

Technical Exercises

In this section you will be required to play a selection of exercises drawn from each of the groups below. The assessor will be looking for the speed of your response and will also give credit for the level of your musicality. Please see the syllabus guide for details on the marking criteria.

- Candidates can choose to play ***either*** natural minor ***or*** harmonic minor scales
- Major and contrary motion scales, minor scales, chromatic scales and arpeggios need to be played hands together, in straight or swung feel, ascending and descending, in the keys, octaves and tempos shown
- Pentatonic scales are right hand only
- Dorian and mixolydian modes need to be played hands separately
- Groups A, B and C (scales, arpeggios and chords) need to be played from memory. You may use your book for Group D (technical studies)

Note that Groups A and B need to be played to a click and any fingerings shown are suggestions only.

Group A: Scales
The tempo for this group is ♩=104 bpm.

1. A♭ major

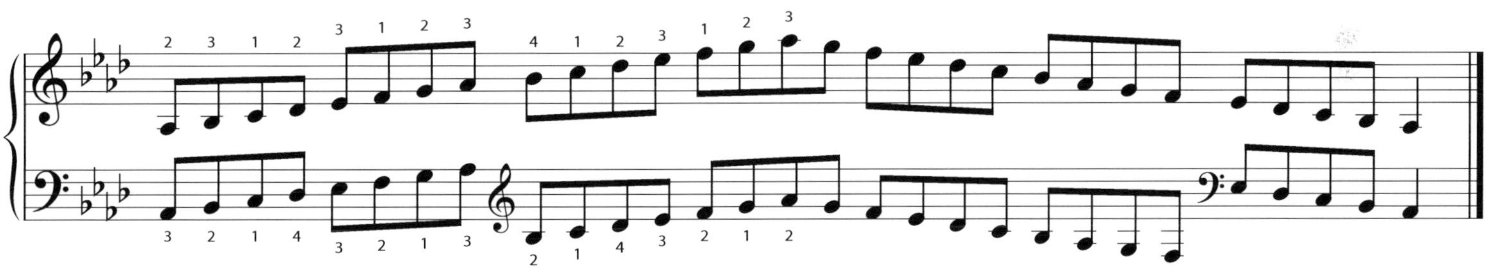

2. A♭ major | contrary motion

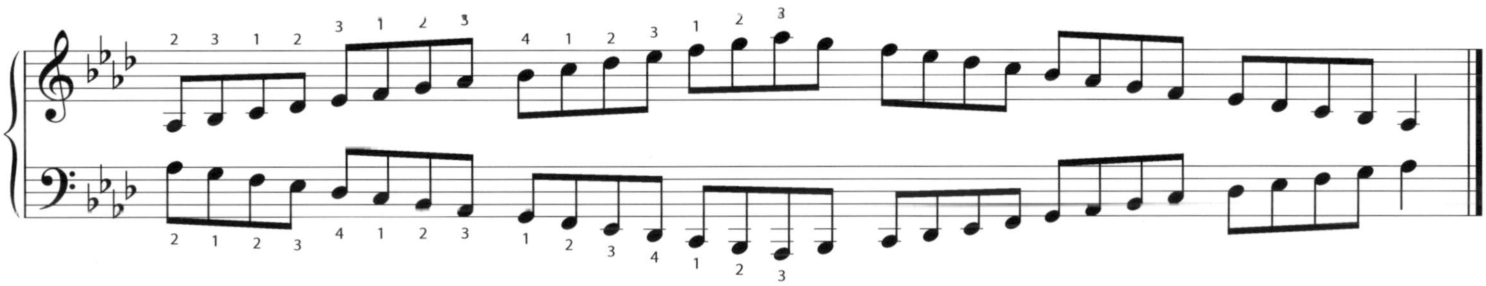

3. E major

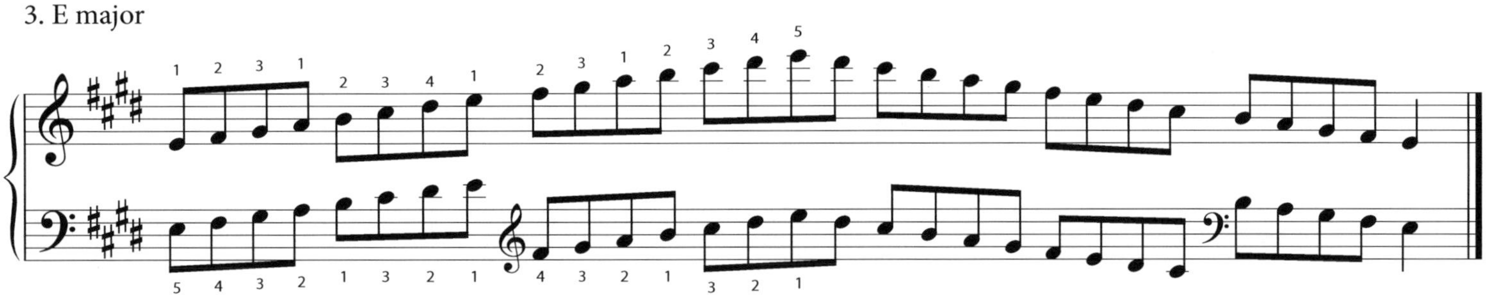

4. E major | contrary motion

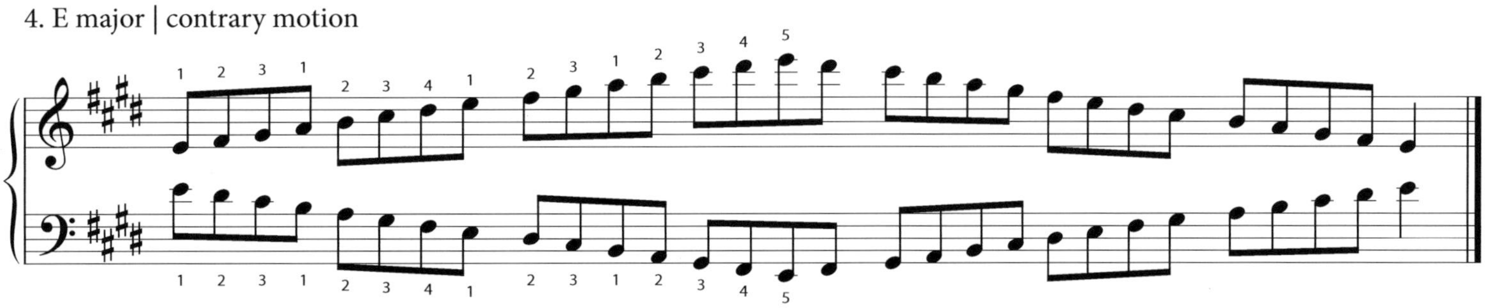

5. F natural minor

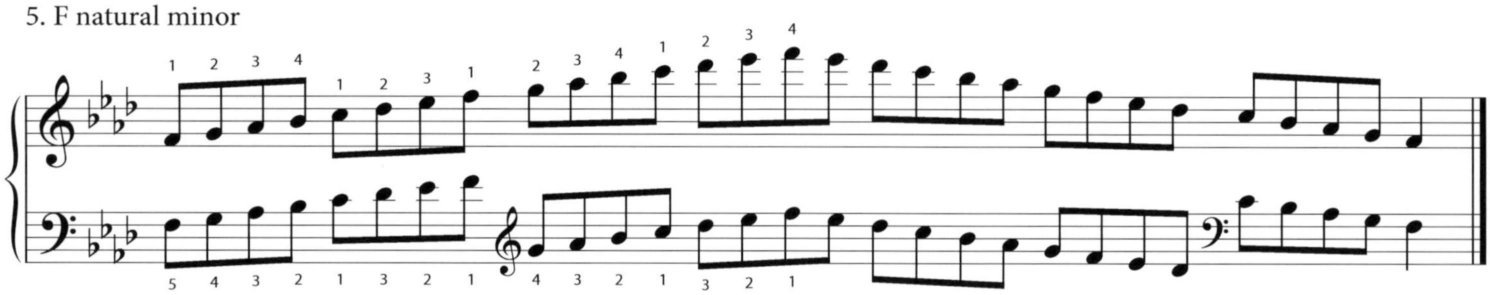

6. C♯ natural minor

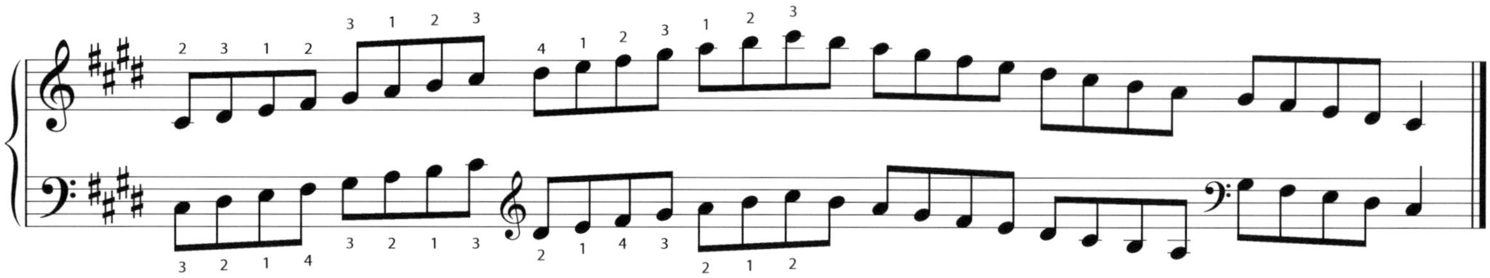

7. F harmonic minor

8. C♯ harmonic Minor

9. A♭ major pentatonic | right hand

10. E major pentatonic | right hand

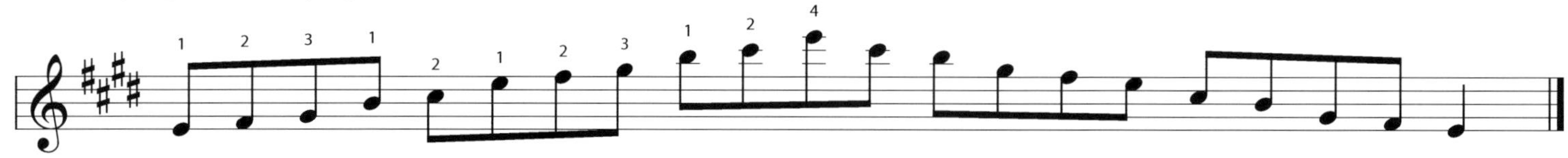

11. F minor pentatonic | right hand

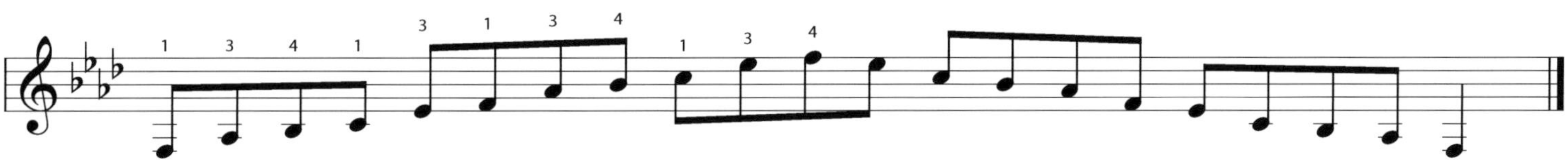

12. C♯ minor pentatonic | right hand

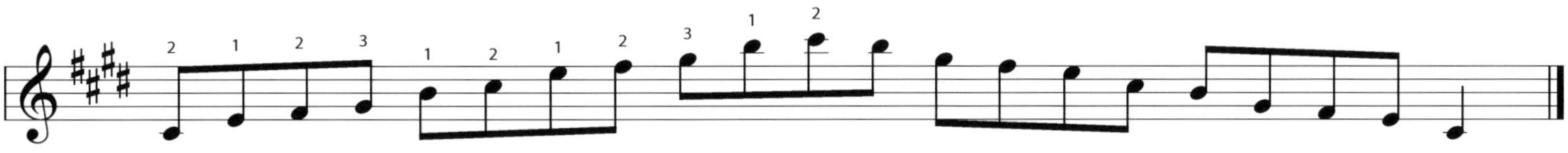

13. C dorian | right hand

14. C dorian | left hand

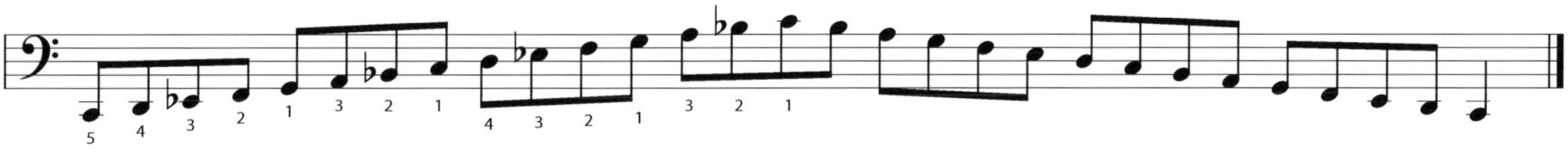

15. C mixolydian | right hand

16. C mixolydian | left hand

17. Chromatic scale | starting on any black key stated by assessor (example given in A♭)

Group B: Arpeggios

The tempo for this group is ♩=76 bpm.

1. A♭ major arpeggio

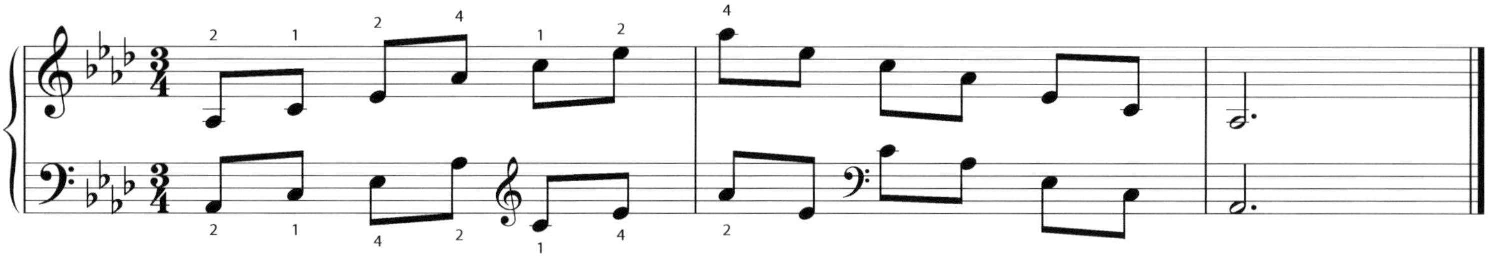

2. E major arpeggio

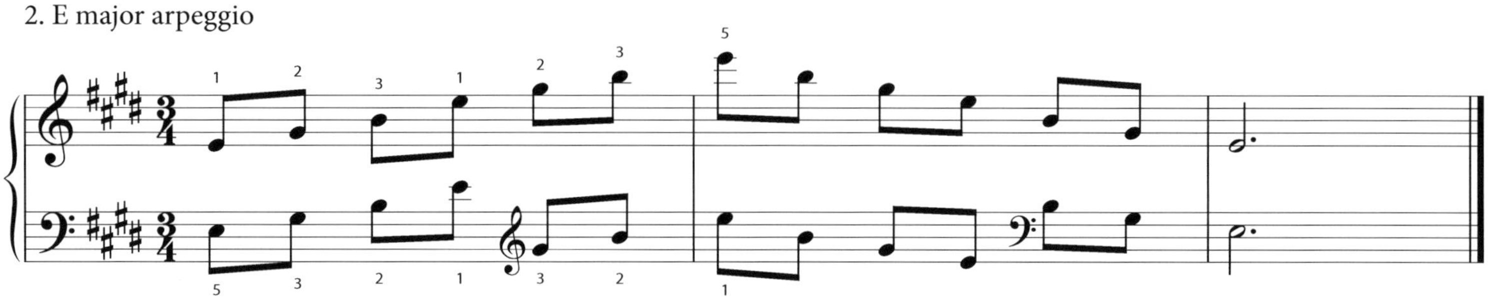

3. F minor arpeggio

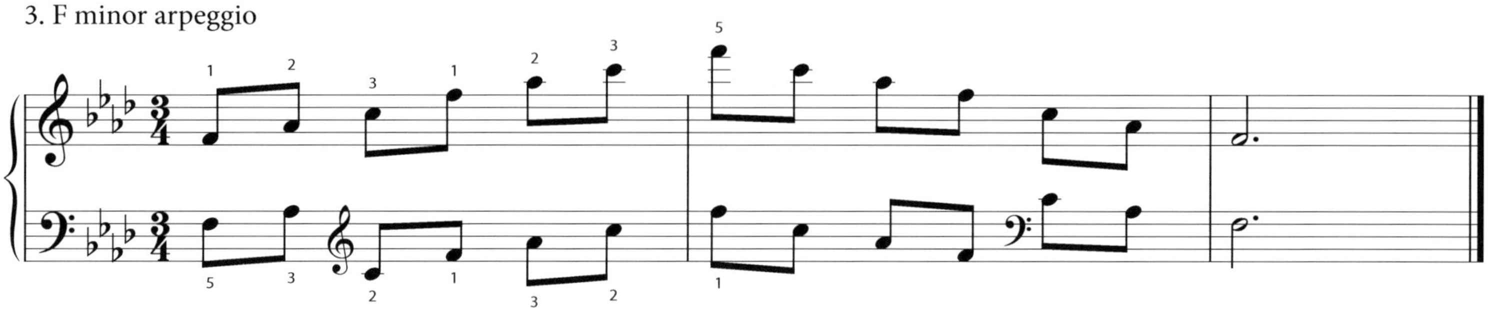

4. C♯ minor arpeggio

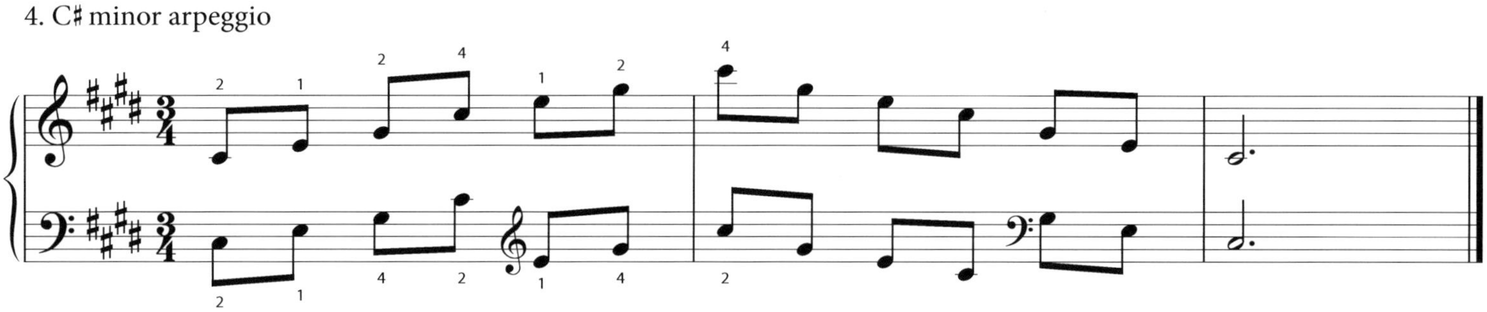

5. C minor 7♭5 ($Cm^{7\flat5}$) or C half-diminished ($C^{\varnothing}$) arpeggio

6. C diminished 7 (C dim^7 or C$^{\circ 7}$) arpeggio

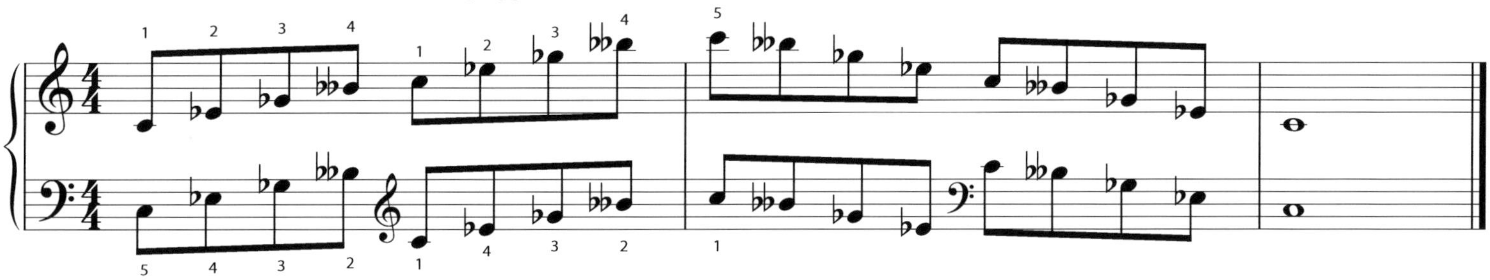

7. C minor 9 | right hand

8. C minor 9 | left hand

9. C dominant 9 | right hand

10. C dominant 9 | left hand

Group C: Chord Voicings

In the assessment you will be asked to play *one of the* chord exercises below, from memory. The assessor will state the chord type. This test is performed in free time (without backing track or click), but the assessor will be looking for the speed of your response.

Ex 1: Major 9th Chords

Ex 2: Dominant 9th Chords

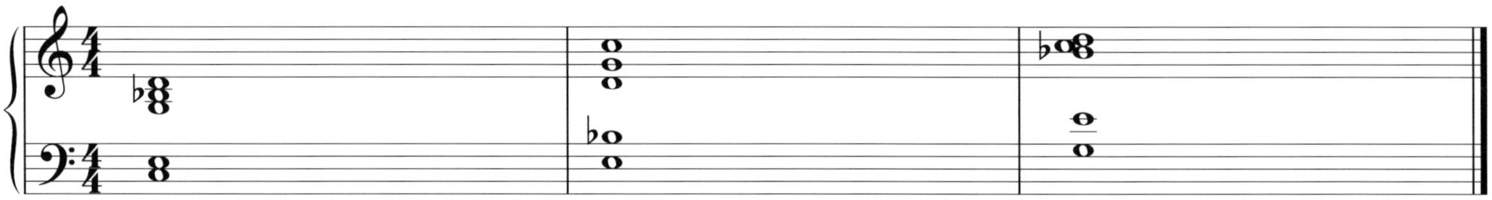

Ex 3: Minor 9th Chords

Group D: Technical Studies

In the assessment you will be asked to perform <u>your choice</u> of *one* of the following three technical studies along with the accompanying backing track.

1. IIm–V–I progressions & walking bass

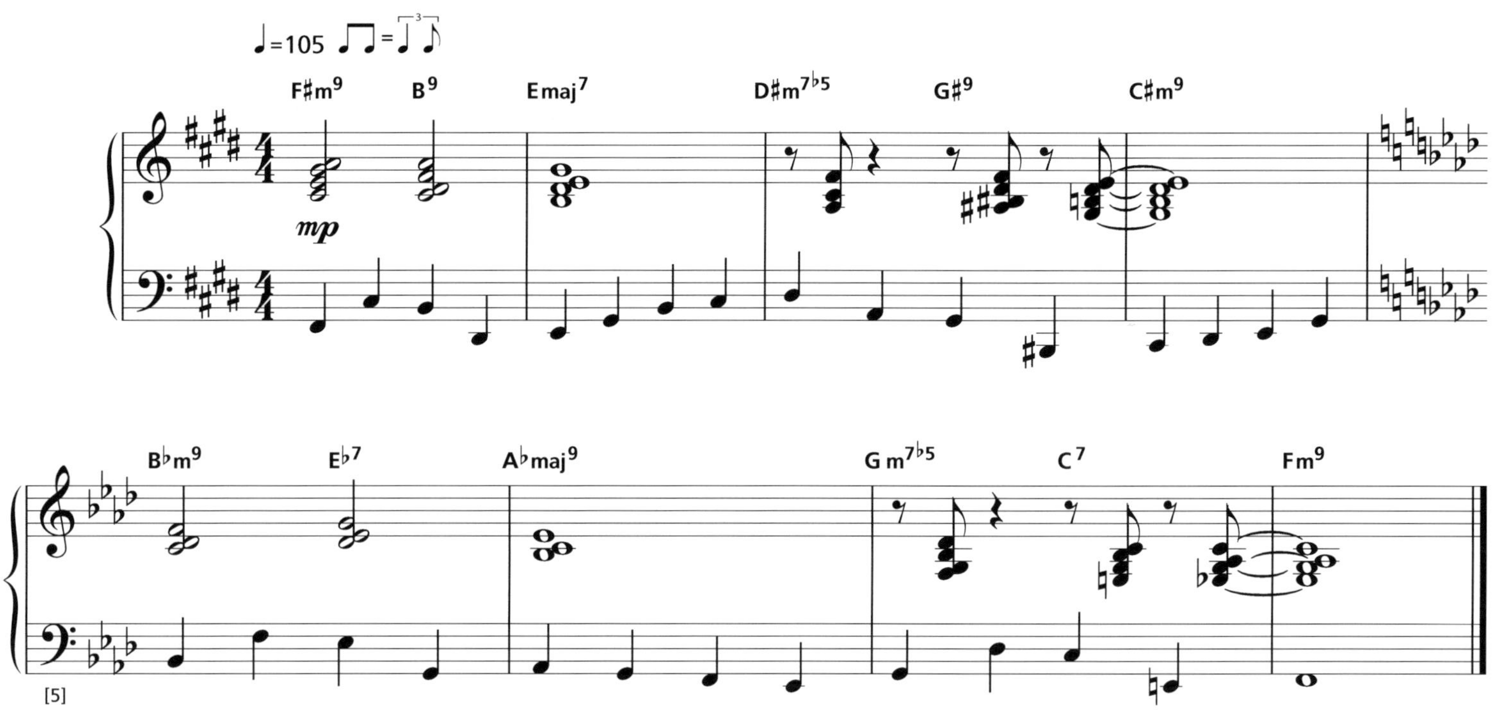

2. Dorian modal study

3. Mixolydian modal study

Sight Reading

In the assessment, you have a choice between either a Sight Reading test or an Improvisation & Interpretation test. The assessor will ask you which one you wish to choose before commencing. Once you have decided you cannot change your mind.

In the sight reading test, the assessor will give you a 8 measure melody in the key of either E major or A♭ major. You will first be given 90 seconds to practise, after which the assessor will play the backing track twice. The first time is for you to practise and the second time is for you to perform the final version for the assessment. For each playthrough, the backing track will begin with a one measure count-in. The tempo is ♩= 60–130.

During the practice time, you will be given the choice of a metronome click throughout or a one measure count in at the beginning.

The backing track is continuous, so once the first playthrough has finished, the count in of the second playing will start immediately.

Sight Reading | Example 1

Please note: The tests shown are examples: The assessor will give you a different version in the assessment

Sight Reading | Example 2

Please note: The tests shown are examples: The assessor will give you a different version in the assessment

Improvisation & Interpretation

In the assessment, you have a choice between either a Sight Reading test or an Improvisation & Interpretation test. The assessor will ask you which one you wish to choose before commencing. Once you have decided you cannot change your mind.

In the Improvisation & Interpretation test, the assessor will give you a 8–12 measure chord progression in the key of either E major or A♭ major. You will first be given 90 seconds to practise, after which the assessor will play the backing track twice. The first time is for you to practise and the second time is for you to perform the final version for the assessment. For each playthrough, the backing track will begin with a one measure count-in. The tempo is ♩=60–130.

During the practice time, you will be given the choice of a metronome click throughout or a one measure count-in at the beginning.

The backing track is continuous, so once the first playthrough has finished, the count-in of the second playing will start immediately.

You will need to improvise diatonic, single note melodies with right hand and chords in left hand.

Improvisation & Interpretation | Example 1

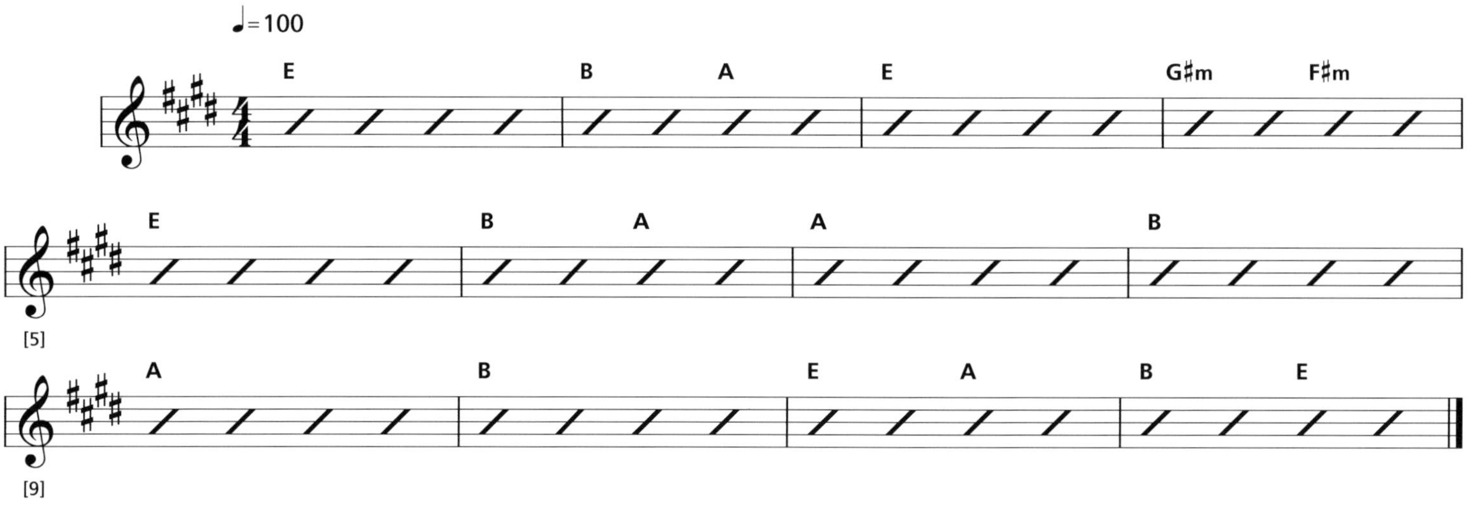

Please note: The test shown is an example: The assessor will give you a different version in the assessment

Improvisation & Interpretation | Example 2

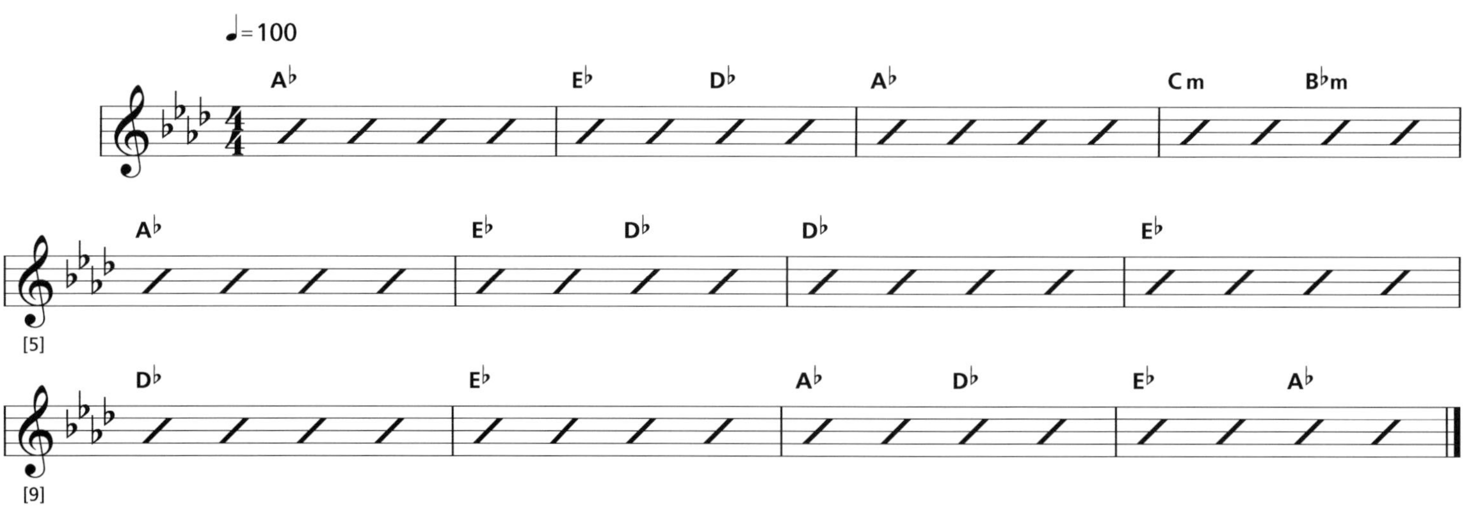

Please note: The test shown is an example: The assessor will give you a different version in the assessment

Ear Tests

In this section, there are two ear tests:

- Melodic Recall
- Harmonic Recall

You will find one example of each type of test printed below and you will need perform both of them in the assessment.

Test 1: Melodic Recall

The assessor will play you a two measure diatonic melody in the key of C major with a range up to a sixth. The first note will be the root note. You will hear the test twice, each time with a one measure count-in, then you will hear a further one measure count-in after which you will need to play the melody to the click. The tempo is ♩=95 bpm.

It is acceptable to play over the track as it is being played as well as practicing after the second playthough. The length of time available after the second playthrough is pre-recorded on the audio track so the count-in may begin while you are still practising.

Please note: The test shown is an example: The assessor will give you a different version in the assessment

Test 2: Harmonic Recall

The assessor will play you a chord progression containing chords I, IV and V in any order or combination in the key of C major. You will hear the chord progression twice, each time with a one measure count-in. You will then hear a further one measure count in before playing back to a click. Please note, there is no requirement for the chords to be voicing-specific. The tempo is ♩=95 bpm.

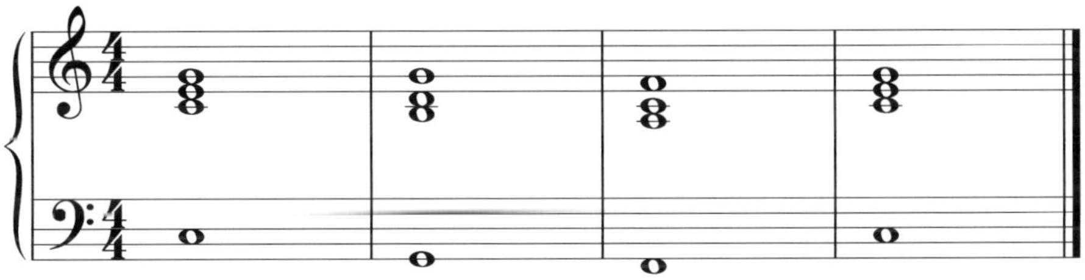

Please note: The test shown is an example: The assessor will give you a different version in the assessment

General Musicianship Questions

The final part of your assessment is the General Musicianship Questions section, which features five questions relating to one of your choice of the performance pieces.

1. You will be asked a question relating to the harmony from a section of one of your pieces
2. You will be asked a question relating to the melody in a section of one of your pieces
3. You will be asked a question relating to the rhythms used in a section of one of your pieces
4. You will be asked a question relating to the technical requirements of one of your pieces
5. You will be asked a question relating to the genre of one of your pieces

Further guidance on the types of questions asked at this level/grade can be found at the RSL website *www.rslawards.com*

Entering Rockschool Assessments

Entering a Rockschool assessment is easy, just go online and follow our simple six step process. All details for entering online, dates, fees, regulations and Free Choice pieces can be found at *www.rslawards.com*

- All candidates should ensure they bring their own Level/Grade syllabus book to the assessment or have proof of digital purchase ready to show the assessor.

- All Level/Grade 6–8 candidates must ensure that they bring valid photo ID to their assessment.

Marking Schemes

Debut to Level/Grade 8

ELEMENT	PASS	MERIT	DISTINCTION
Performance Piece 1	12–14 out of 20	15–17 out of 20	18+ out of 20
Performance Piece 2	12–14 out of 20	15–17 out of 20	18+ out of 20
Performance Piece 3	12–14 out of 20	15–17 out of 20	18+ out of 20
Technical Exercises	9–10 out of 15	11–12 out of 15	13+ out of 15
Sight Reading *or* Improvisation & Interpretation	6 out of 10	7–8 out of 10	9+ out of 10
Ear Tests	6 out of 10	7–8 out of 10	9+ out of 10
General Musicianship Questions	3 out of 5	4 out of 5	5 out of 5
TOTAL MARKS	60%+	74%+	90%+

Performance Certificates | Debut to Level/Grade 8

ELEMENT	PASS	MERIT	DISTINCTION
Performance Piece 1	12–14 out of 20	15–17 out of 20	18+ out of 20
Performance Piece 2	12–14 out of 20	15–17 out of 20	18+ out of 20
Performance Piece 3	12–14 out of 20	15–17 out of 20	18+ out of 20
Performance Piece 4	12–14 out of 20	15–17 out of 20	18+ out of 20
Performance Piece 5	12–14 out of 20	15–17 out of 20	18+ out of 20
TOTAL MARKS	60%+	75%+	90%+

Copyright Information

Piano Notation Explained

THE MUSICAL STAVE shows pitches and rhythms and is divided by lines into measures. Pitches are named after the first seven letters of the alphabet.

Grace Note: Play the grace note on or before the beat depending on the style of music, then move quickly to the note it leads onto.

Pedal Marking: Depress and then release the sustain pedal. Multiple pedal operations in a short space of time may be simplified as shown in the last two beats of the measure below.

Spread Chord: Play the chord from the bottom note up (top down only if there is a downward arrow head). The final note should sound by the appropriate notated measure position.

Glissando: Play the notes between the notated pitches by sliding over the keyboard with the fingers or fingernails.

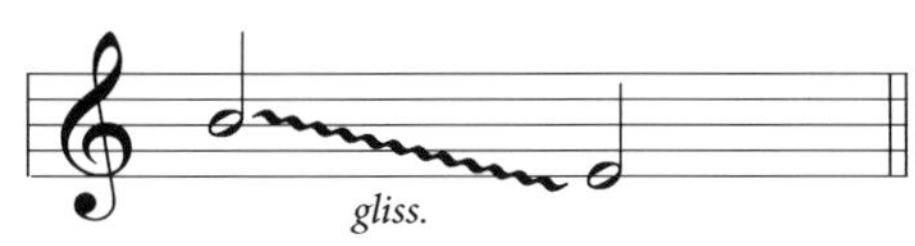

Tremolando: Oscillate at speed between marked notes.

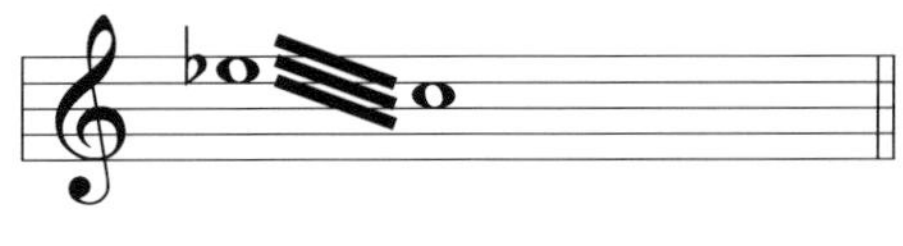

Finger Markings: These numbers represent your fingers. 1 is the thumb, 2 the index finger and so on.

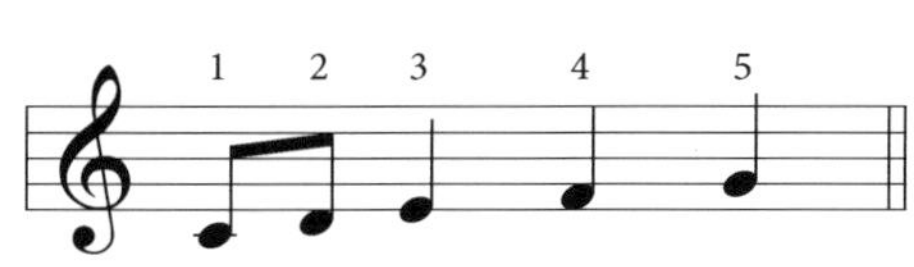

 (accent) • Accentuate note (play it louder).

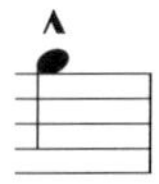 (accent) • Accentuate note with great intensity.

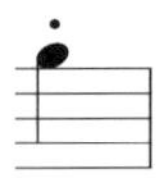 (staccato) • Shorten time value of note.

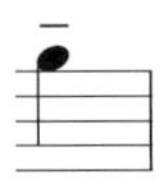 (accent) • Accentuate note with more arm weight.

D.𝄋. al Coda • Go back to the sign (𝄋), then play until the measure marked ***To Coda*** 𝄌 then skip to the section marked 𝄌 ***Coda***.

D.C. al Fine • Go back to the beginning of the song and play until the measure marked ***Fine*** (end).

Una Corda • Use soft pedal

 • Repeat the measures between the repeat signs.

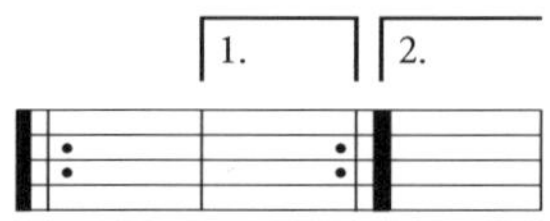

• When a repeated section has different endings, play the first ending only the first time and the second ending only the second time.